Contents

How to use this book

Each page has a title telling you what it is about.

Read the word problems very carefully. Decide how you will work out the answers.

Instructions look like this. Always read these carefully before starting.

This shows you how to set out your work. The first question is done for you.

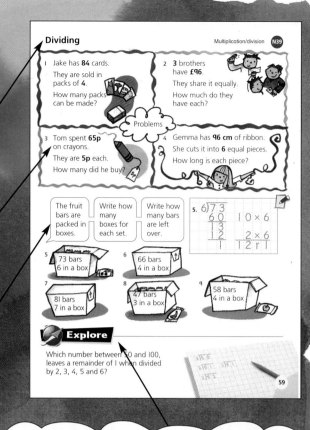

This shows that the activity is an **Explore**. Work with a friend.

Ask your teacher if you need to do these.

This means you decide how to set out your work and show your workings.

Sometimes there is a **Hint** to help you.

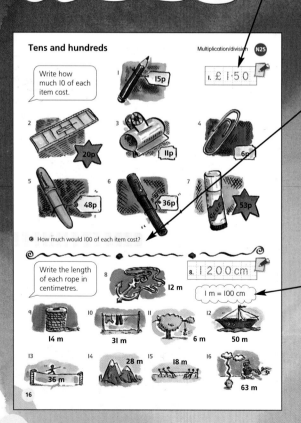

Sometimes you need materials to help you.

Counting in 2s

Write the next 6 numbers.

1. 2 2, 2 4, 2 6, 2 8, 3 0, 3 2

 1 16, 18, 20, …

 2 28, 30, 32, …

 3 40, 42, 44, …

 4 6, 8, 10, …

 5 58, 56, 54, …

 6 16, 14, 12, …

 7 34, 36, 38, …

 8 70, 72, 74, …

 9 90, 88, 86, …

Choose the yo-yos that are multiples of 2.

Write them in order, smallest to largest.

Write the next multiple of 5.

I. 72

I. **7 5**

2 99

3 37

4 24

5 63

6 58

7 12

8 16

9 27

10 32

II 69

12 78

13 84

14 7

15 II

16 95

17 41

e Write the next multiple of I0.

Copy the grid and circle the multiples of 5.

Put a square around the multiples of I0.

31	32	33	34	35	36	37	38	39	40
41	42	43	44	45	46	47	48	49	50
51	52	53	54	55	56	57	58	59	60
61	62	63	64	65	66	67	68	69	70

Counting in 3s and 4s

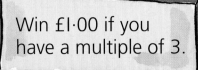

Win £1·00 if you have a multiple of 3.

Win 50p if you have a multiple of 4.

Write how much each child wins.

1

16   44
18   27
32

1. £3·50

2

20   15
17   42
33

3

19   9
28   45
100

4

40   17
63   80
8

5

4   39
30   52
10

6

21   68
14   6
64

7

3   41
51   22
56

📧 Write some numbers which are multiples of 3 **and** 4.

 **Explore**

Find the smallest number that is a multiple of

2   3   4   5   and   10 .

5

Sixes

Write how many doughnuts in total.

1

i. $4 \times 6 = 24$

2

3

4

5

6

7

8

9

10

Copy and complete.

11   $4 \times 6 =$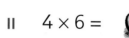

ii. $4 \times 6 = 24$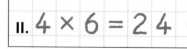

12   $3 \times 6 =$

13   $5 \times 6 =$

14   $2 \times 6 =$

15   $7 \times 6 =$

16   $10 \times 6 =$

17   $8 \times 6 =$

18   $6 \times 6 =$

19   $1 \times 6 =$

20   $9 \times 6 =$

6

e Write the first twelve multiples of 6 in order.

Sixes

> Each box holds 6 cans.

> Write the number of boxes needed.

1

36 cans

1. $36 \div 6 = 6$

2
12 cans

3
60 cans

4
24 cans

5
30 cans

6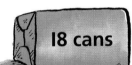
18 cans

7
42 cans

8
48 cans

9
66 cans

10
54 cans

---

e How many boxes if each one holds 3 cans?

> Copy and complete.

11   $3 \times 6 =$

ii. $3 \times 6 = 18$

12   $7 \times 6 =$

13    $\div 6 = 10$

14   $5 \times 6 =$

15   $18 \div 6 =$

16    $\div 6 = 1$

17   $36 \div 6 =$

18   $9 \times 6 =$

19   $30 \div 6 =$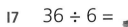

20   $54 \div 6 =$

21   $6 \times 6 =$

22    $\div 6 = 4$

23    $\times 6 = 42$

7

Write the total for each set of stickers.

Prices

star stickers 3p

animal stickers 6p

1. $2 \times 3\,p = 6\,p$

$3 \times 6\,p = 18\,p$

$6\,p + 18\,p = 24\,p$

1

2

3

4

5

6

7

8

ℯ What are the possible prices for 10 stickers?

Explore

Choose a number in the ×6 table.

Choose a number in the ×3 table.

Take the smaller number away from the larger number.

Repeat several times.

What do you notice about the answers?

$18 - 3 = 15$
$24 - 6 = 18$
$6 - 3 =$

Nines

Copy and complete.

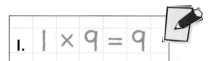

I. $1 \times 9 = 9$

I.

$1 \times 9 =$

2

$2 \times 9 =$

3

$3 \times 9 =$

4

$4 \times 9 =$

5

$5 \times 9 =$

6

$6 \times 9 =$

7

$7 \times 9 =$

8

$8 \times 9 =$

9

$9 \times 9 =$

10

$10 \times 9 =$

Each bag holds 9 cherries.

Write how many cherries in total.

II.

II. $4 \times 9 = 36$

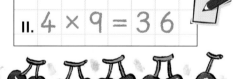

12

13

14

15

16

17

18

19

Nines

A hit is worth 9 points.

Write the number of hits.

45 points

I. $45 \div 9 = 5$

2 **27 points**

3 **9 points**

4 **90 points**

5 **63 points**

6 **18 points**

7 **54 points**

8 **36 points**

9 **72 points**

10 **81 points**

Each cat has 9 lives.

Write how many lives for each set.

2 cats

II. $2 \times 9 = 18$

5 cats

4 cats

9 cats

7 cats

8 cats

10 cats

3 cats

6 cats

Explore

Use the number cards shown.

Make 5 different numbers from the ×9 table using all the cards.

0 1 2 3 4 5 6 7 8 9

Copy and complete.

ı. $2 \times 9 = 18, \quad 1 + 8 = 9$

	×9 table		adding the digits	
1	$2 \times 9 =$	18	$1 + 8 =$	
2	$3 \times 9 =$			
3	$4 \times 9 =$			
4	$5 \times 9 =$			
5	$6 \times 9 =$			
6	$7 \times 9 =$			
7	$8 \times 9 =$			
8	$9 \times 9 =$			
9	$10 \times 9 =$			

℮ Find the difference between the digits in each answer. Write about the patterns.

Copy and complete. Write about the pattern.

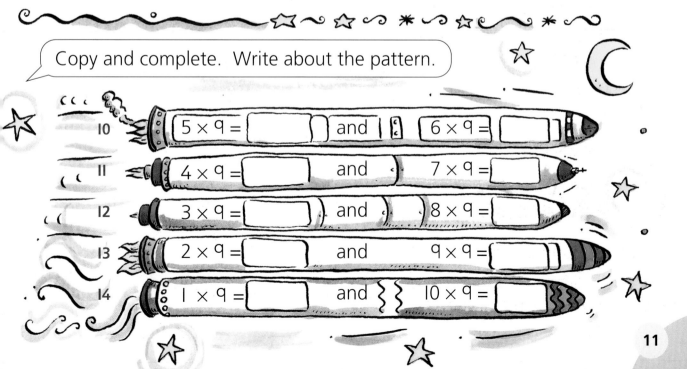

10 $5 \times 9 = \boxed{}$ and $6 \times 9 = \boxed{}$

11 $4 \times 9 = \boxed{}$ and $7 \times 9 = \boxed{}$

12 $3 \times 9 = \boxed{}$ and $8 \times 9 = \boxed{}$

13 $2 \times 9 = \boxed{}$ and $9 \times 9 = \boxed{}$

14 $1 \times 9 = \boxed{}$ and $10 \times 9 = \boxed{}$

Sevens

Write the number of days to reach each planet.

1

4 weeks

I. $4 \times 7 = 28$ days

I week = 7 days

2

2 weeks

3

I week

4

6 weeks

5

8 weeks

6

7 weeks

7

9 weeks

8

5 weeks

9

II weeks

10

10 weeks

11

3 weeks

12

12 weeks

13

13 weeks

Copy and complete.

14   $4 \times 7 =$

14. $4 \times 7 = 28$

15   $5 \times 7 =$

16   $2 \times 7 =$

17   $10 \times 7 =$

18   $3 \times 7 =$

19   $6 \times 7 =$

20   $11 \times 7 =$

21   $8 \times 7 =$

22   $7 \times 7 =$

23   $9 \times 7 =$

Sevens

How many weeks to each birthday?

1

14 days

I. $14 \div 7 = 2$ weeks

2

28 days

3

42 days

4

49 days

5

63 days

6

35 days

7

21 days

8

70 days

9

56 days

🅮 Find out how many weeks until your birthday.

Copy and complete.

10 $42 \div 7 =$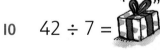

10. $42 \div 7 = 6$

11 $14 \div 7 =$

12 $28 \div 7 =$

13 $70 \div 7 =$

14 $21 \div 7 =$

15 $7 \div 7 =$

16 $35 \div 7 =$

17 $56 \div 7 =$

18 $49 \div 7 =$

19 $63 \div 7 =$

🅮 Write the multiplication for each division.

Copy and complete the multiplication square.

Write the numbers that appear most often on the grid.

Write the numbers that appear only once.

1	2	3	4	5	6	7	8	9	10
2	4	6	8	10					
3	6	9	12	15					
4	8	12							
5	10	15							
6	12	18							
7	14	21							
8	16	24							
9	18	27							
10	20	30							

Copy and complete.

1  $\times 7 = 14$

1. $2 \times 7 = 14$

2 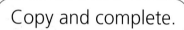 $\times 7 = 35$

3 $\div 7 = 3$

4 $\div 7 = 5$

5 $\div 7 = 6$

6 $\times 7 = 63$

7 $7 \div$ $= 1$

8 $8 \times 7 =$

9 $\times 7 = 28$

10 $\div 7 = 11$

Explore

Write out the multiples of 7 up to 20×7.

Add the digits of each number.

Continue adding until you reach a 1-digit

Can you find a pattern?

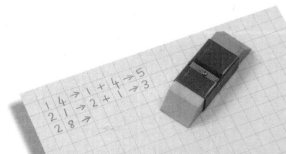

Tens and hundreds

> Each banana costs 10p.

> Write how much for each group.

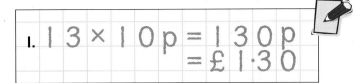

I. $13 \times 10p = 130p$
$= £1·30$

1

13 bananas

2

19 bananas

3

23 bananas

4

10 bananas

5

21 bananas

6

30 bananas

7

22 bananas

8

16 bananas

q

15 bananas

> How many bananas could you buy with these amounts?

10  £3·50

10. 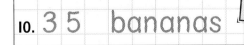 3 5 bananas

11  10p

12 £1·00 13 £4·80 14 £2·80 15 £5·60 16 £4·20

Tens and hundreds

Write how much 10 of each item cost.

1 15p

1. £1·50

2  20p

3  11p

4  6p

5  48p

6  36p

7  53p

🅔 How much would 100 of each item cost?

Write the length of each rope in centimetres.

8  12 m

8. 1200 cm

1 m = 100 cm

9  14 m

10  31 m

11  6 m

12  50 m

13  36 m

14  28 m

15  18 m

16  63 m

16

Tens and hundreds

> Nails are sold in boxes of 100.

> Write how many boxes are needed.

1. $400 \div 100 = 4 \text{ boxes}$

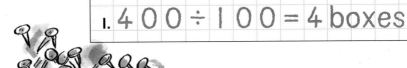

1

400 nails

2  **300 nails**

3 **900 nails**

4 **6000 nails**

5 **2500 nails**

6 **800 nails**

7 **7200 nails**

> Copy and complete.

8. $70 \times 10 = 700$

8 $70 \times 10 = $

9 $3 \times 100 = $

10 $700 \div 10 = $

11 $1000 \div 100 = $

12 $9000 \div 10 = $

13 $24 \times 10 = $

14 $40 \times 100 = $

15 $800 \div 100 = $

16 $4000 \div 10 = $

Problems

17a Tim saves **10p** coins. He has **£7·80**. How many **10p** coins?

b His aunt gives him **15** more **10p** coins. How much now?

c He buys a computer magazine for **£3·99**. How much does he have left?

17

Multiplying

There are 3 children in each family.

I. $3 \times 30p = 90p$

They each get the pocket money shown.

Write how much in total.

2

3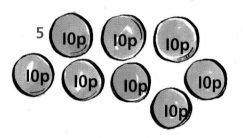

4

5

6

7

Write how much if there are 4 children.

Ia. $4 \times 30p = 120p$

Write how much if there are 2 children.

Ib. $2 \times 30p = 60p$

Write the cost of each set of stamps.

8

8. $2 \times 10p = 20p$

9

10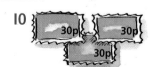

11

12

13

14

15

16

18

Multiplying

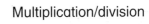

Mr Currant bakes buns in rows of 4.

Write how many on each tray.

1  22 rows

2  24 rows

1.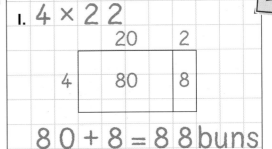
$$4 \times 22$$

	20	2
4	80	8

$$80 + 8 = 88 \text{ buns}$$

3  32 rows

4  15 rows

5  26 rows

6  19 rows

7 41 rows

8  23 rows

9  36 rows

10 34 rows

11  11 rows

---

Copy and complete.

12.
	20	1
2	40	2

$$2 \times 21 = 40 + 2 = 42$$

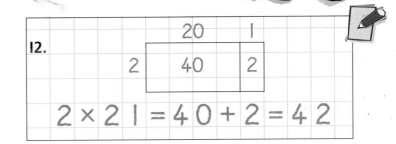

12 $2 \times 21 = $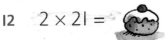

13 $3 \times 24 = $  14 $4 \times 31 = $ 15 $5 \times 26 = $ 16 $4 \times 24 = $

17 $6 \times 23 = $ 18 $2 \times 43 = $ 19 $3 \times 22 = $ 20 $5 \times 33 = $

21 $7 \times 24 = $ 22 $8 \times 42 = $ 23 $5 \times 51 = $ 24 $9 \times 15 = $

25 $6 \times 36 = $ 26 $3 \times 34 = $ 27 $4 \times 35 = $ 28 $2 \times 32 = $

Multiplying

Josh and Elsa do lots of jobs.

Write how much they earn.

post letter	24p	wash window	53p
walk dog	42p	wash up	31p
empty bin	13p	wash car	62p

1
walk 2 dogs

$$1.\ 2 \times 42p = 84p$$

2
post 8 letters

3
wash 5 windows

4
wash up 4 times

5
wash 3 cars

6
empty 9 bins

7
wash 4 windows

8
post 5 letters

9
wash 7 cars

10
walk 4 dogs

11
empty 3 bins

12
wash up 7 times

13
post 9 letters

Explore

How many different multiplications can you find to match this?

How many can you find to make 144?

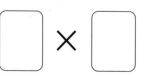 × = **120**

6 × 20
2 × 60

Fractions

Write the coloured part of each strip as a fraction.

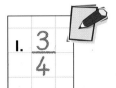

1. $\dfrac{3}{4}$

1

2

3

4

5

6

Write the smaller fraction.

7 $\dfrac{1}{4}$ $\dfrac{1}{8}$

Use the strips at the top of the page.

7. $\dfrac{1}{8}$

8 $\dfrac{1}{6}$ $\dfrac{1}{4}$

9 $\dfrac{1}{10}$ $\dfrac{1}{9}$

10 $\dfrac{1}{8}$ $\dfrac{1}{6}$

11 $\dfrac{3}{4}$ $\dfrac{1}{2}$

12 $\dfrac{2}{5}$ $\dfrac{5}{9}$

13 $\dfrac{5}{6}$ $\dfrac{3}{4}$

Write the larger fraction.

14 $\dfrac{4}{5}$ $\dfrac{9}{10}$

15 $\dfrac{4}{6}$ $\dfrac{1}{2}$

16 $\dfrac{7}{9}$ $\dfrac{1}{2}$

17 $\dfrac{3}{4}$ $\dfrac{6}{10}$

18 $\dfrac{5}{8}$ $\dfrac{1}{2}$

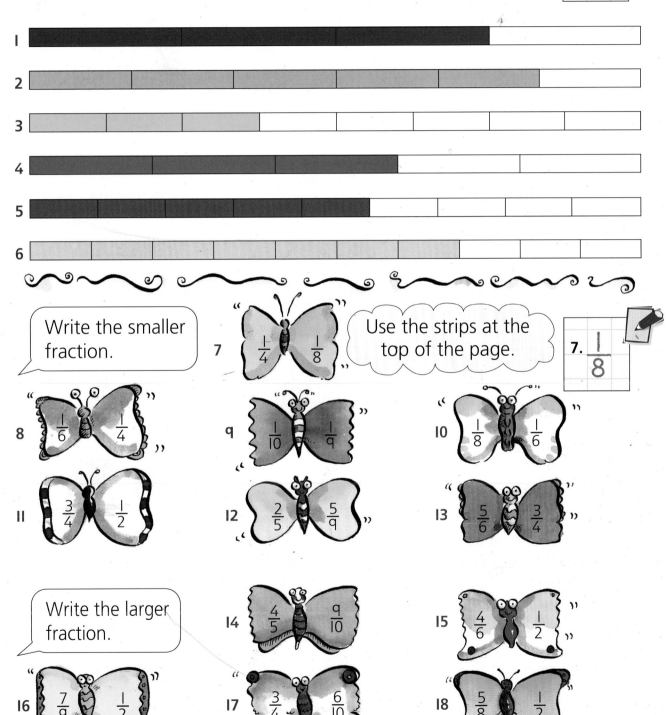

e Write all the fractions in order, smallest to largest.

Write the amount to be eaten as a fraction.

1

1. $\dfrac{3}{8}$

2

3

4

5

6

7

8

9

10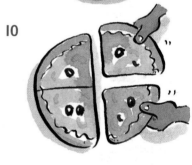

Compare each amount with $\frac{1}{2}$.

Use '<', '>' or '='.

1a. $\dfrac{3}{8} < \dfrac{1}{2}$

Explore

$\dfrac{3}{6}$ This fraction is equal to $\frac{1}{2}$.
Write 5 more like this.

$\dfrac{1}{10}$ This fraction is less than $\frac{1}{2}$.
Write 5 more like this.

$\dfrac{7}{8}$ This fraction is more than $\frac{1}{2}$.
Write 5 more like this.

Fractions

Write the fraction shown.

a. $\dfrac{1}{3}$

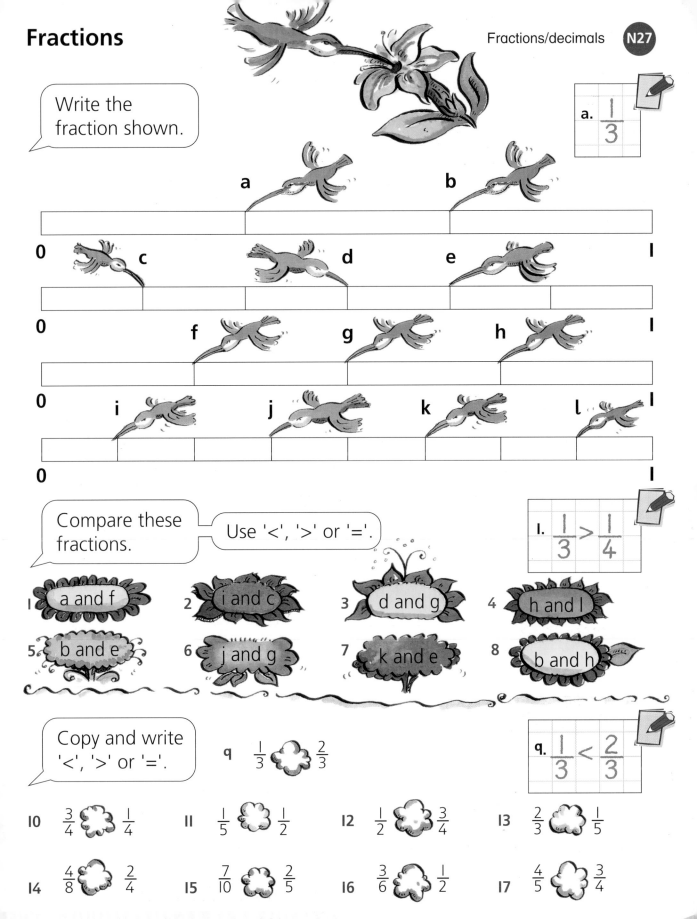

Compare these fractions.

Use '<', '>' or '='.

l. $\dfrac{1}{3} > \dfrac{1}{4}$

1 a and f
2 i and c
3 d and g
4 h and l
5 b and e
6 j and g
7 k and e
8 b and h

Copy and write '<', '>' or '='.

q $\dfrac{1}{3}$ 🌸 $\dfrac{2}{3}$

q. $\dfrac{1}{3} < \dfrac{2}{3}$

10 $\dfrac{3}{4}$ 🌸 $\dfrac{1}{4}$

11 $\dfrac{1}{5}$ 🌸 $\dfrac{1}{2}$

12 $\dfrac{1}{2}$ 🌸 $\dfrac{3}{4}$

13 $\dfrac{2}{3}$ 🌸 $\dfrac{1}{5}$

14 $\dfrac{4}{8}$ 🌸 $\dfrac{2}{4}$

15 $\dfrac{7}{10}$ 🌸 $\dfrac{2}{5}$

16 $\dfrac{3}{6}$ 🌸 $\dfrac{1}{2}$

17 $\dfrac{4}{5}$ 🌸 $\dfrac{3}{4}$

℮ Make up some fraction pairs of your own.

Fractions

Copy and complete.

I. $\frac{1}{4}$ of 12p = 3p

1 $\frac{1}{4}$ of 12p = ☁

2 $\frac{2}{4}$ of 12p = ☁

3 $\frac{3}{4}$ of 12p = ☁

4 $\frac{4}{4}$ of 12p = ☁

5 $\frac{1}{3}$ of 15p = ☁

6 $\frac{2}{3}$ of 15p = ☁

7 $\frac{3}{3}$ of 15p = ☁

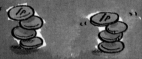

8 $\frac{1}{5}$ of 20p = ☁

9 $\frac{2}{5}$ of 20p = ☁

10 $\frac{3}{5}$ of 20p = ☁

11 $\frac{4}{5}$ of 20p = ☁

12 $\frac{5}{5}$ of 20p = ☁

ℓ Use 24 1p coins. Write some amounts as fractions.

Explore

Use 10p coins.

Make **equal** piles.

Write different fractions.

$\frac{1}{3}$ of 90p = 30p

Fractions

Write how many marbles in the fraction shown.

1  $\frac{1}{4}$

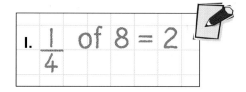

I. $\frac{1}{4}$ of 8 = 2

2  $\frac{1}{3}$

3 $\frac{3}{8}$

4  $\frac{3}{4}$

5  $\frac{2}{5}$

6  $\frac{2}{3}$

7  $\frac{2}{3}$

8  $\frac{5}{6}$

9  $\frac{1}{4}$

10  $\frac{4}{5}$

℮ Write the fraction of marbles that are red.

Copy and complete.

11 $\frac{1}{3}$ of 9 =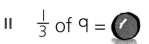

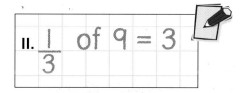

II. $\frac{1}{3}$ of 9 = 3

12 $\frac{1}{4}$ of 8 = ◯

13 $\frac{2}{4}$ of 8 = ◯

Counters

14 $\frac{3}{4}$ of 8 = ◯

15 $\frac{1}{3}$ of 6 = ●

16 $\frac{2}{3}$ of 6 = ●

17 $\frac{3}{3}$ of 6 = ●

18 $\frac{1}{2}$ of 12 = ●

19 $\frac{2}{4}$ of 12 = ●

Fractions

Write the fraction and number of cubes that are red.

1. $\dfrac{2}{3}$ of 12 = 8

2.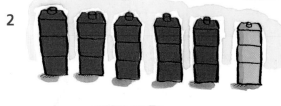

3.

4.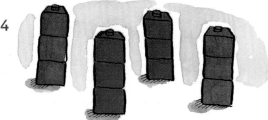

5.

6.

7.

8.

✏ Write the fraction and number of cubes that are multicoloured.

Problems

9. Grandpa has a barrel of apples.

$\dfrac{2}{5}$ are rotten.

24 are good.

How many apples in total?

10. Mon has **£24**.

He gives $\dfrac{1}{2}$ to his brother.

He gives $\dfrac{1}{4}$ to his friend.

He spends $\dfrac{1}{6}$ on a cassette.

How much money has he given each time?
How much money is left?

Rounding

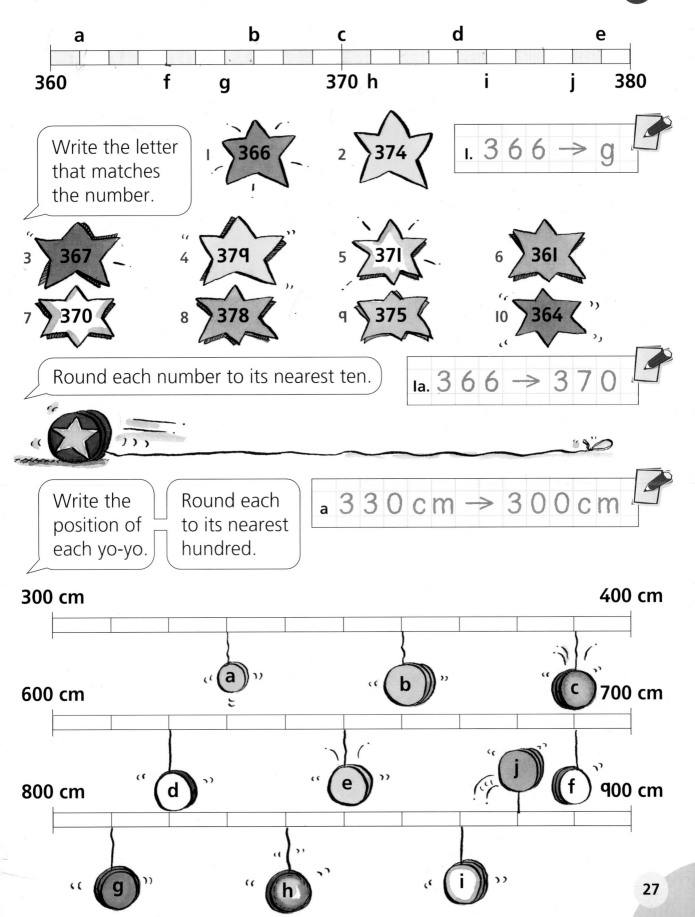

Write the letter that matches the number.

1. 366 → g

2. 374

3. 367

4. 379

5. 371

6. 361

7. 370

8. 378

9. 375

10. 364

Round each number to its nearest ten.

1a. 366 → 370

Write the position of each yo-yo. Round each to its nearest hundred.

a 330 cm → 300 cm

Rounding

Write the position of each pointer.

1. 2 5 8 g

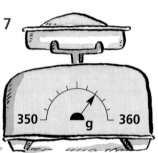

Round each answer to the nearest 10 g.

Round each answer to the nearest 100 g.

1a. 2 5 8 g → 2 6 0 g
    2 5 8 g → 3 0 0 g

Explore

Use the number cards shown.

Make different 3-digit numbers.

Round each number to its nearest ten.

Round each number to its nearest hundred.

How many nearest hundreds are there?

4 2 7

Rounding

Write how many pence in each set.

1

1. 346p

2

3

4

5

6

7

8

9

10

Round each amount to the nearest 10p and the nearest pound.

1. 346p → 350p

346p → 300p → £3

Explore

Write all the numbers with 460 as the nearest ten.

Write 10 numbers with 700 as the nearest hundred.

How many answers are there altogether?

Adding two numbers

Estimate. Copy and complete.

1
```
  H T U
  2 2 6
+ 1 8 0
───────
```

2
```
  H T U
  4 1 6
+ 3 7 5
───────
```

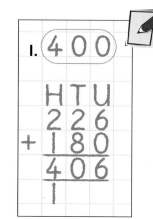

1. 400
```
  H T U
  2 2 6
+ 1 8 0
───────
  4 0 6
  1
```

3
```
  H T U
  1 7 5
+ 2 3 6
───────
```

4
```
  H T U
  2 4 4
+ 3 6 7
───────
```

5
```
  H T U
  3 6 4
+ 1 3 8
───────
```

6
```
  H T U
  3 3 3
+ 5 7 9
───────
```

7
```
  H T U
  5 6 5
+ 2 3 6
───────
```

8
```
  H T U
  1 0 9
+ 4 6 3
───────
```

9
```
  H T U
  2 7 7
+ 5 2 4
───────
```

Each submarine dives 158 m.

Estimate then write the new depths.

10. 450 m
```
  H T U
  2 8 3
+ 1 5 8
───────
  4 4 1 m
  1 1
```

10

283 m

11

294 m

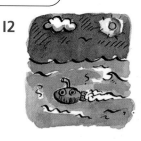

12

178 m

13

227 m

14

199 m

15

285 m

16

207 m

Adding 3-digit numbers

How much in total?

1.  255 g Flour 375 g

2.  341 g Rasins 489 g

3.  248 g 367 g

4.  371 g Peanuts 299 g

5.  176 g Sugar 265 g

6.  353 g Butter 448 g

7.  527 g 366 g

8.  234 g Brown Sugar 259 g

9.  619 g 191 g

10.  355 g Marzipan 455 g

---

Write pairs that add to exactly 500.

 402

 226

 236

 274

 178

 264

 322

 244

 256

 358

 142

 98

Adding 3-digit numbers

Write the total runs for each team.

Estimate first.

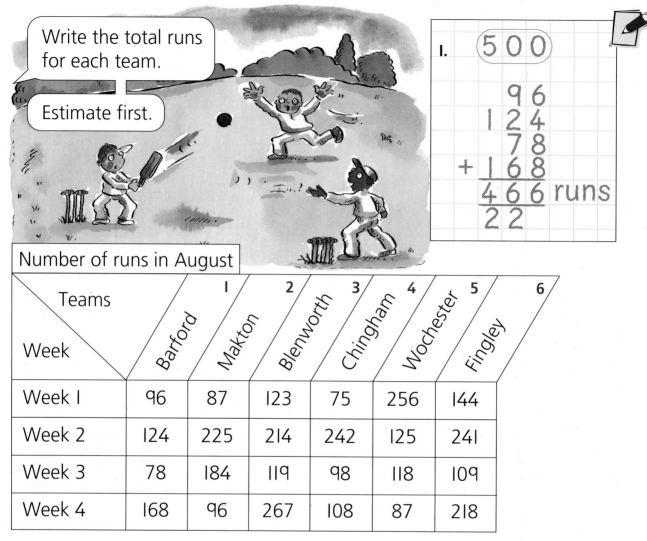

I.
$$\begin{array}{r} 500 \\ 96 \\ 124 \\ 78 \\ +\ 168 \\ \hline 466 \text{ runs} \\ 22 \end{array}$$

Number of runs in August

Week \ Teams	Barford 1	Makton 2	Blenworth 3	Chingham 4	Wochester 5	Fingley 6
Week 1	96	87	123	75	256	144
Week 2	124	225	214	242	125	241
Week 3	78	184	119	98	118	109
Week 4	168	96	267	108	87	218

Explore

Use number cards 1 to 9.

Pick 6 cards and make two 3-digit numbers like this:

2 4 5 + 3 7 1

Add the two numbers.

Score a point for each 0 in your answer.

What is the highest score you can get?

What is your score after 10 turns?

A computer virus subtracts 80 points from each score.

Write the new scores.

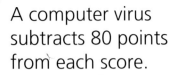

I

I. $367 - 80 = 287$

2
SCORE 256

3
SCORE 373

4
SCORE 552

5
SCORE 147

6
SCORE 608

7
SCORE 431

8
SCORE 824

q
SCORE 912

℮ Another 50 points are subtracted. Write the final scores.

Copy and complete.

I0. $374 - 80 = 294$

10
374 – 80

II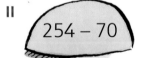
254 – 70

12 171 – 90

13
554 – 60

14 333 – 60

15
742 – 80

16
681 – 90

17
625 – 70

18 423 – 50

19
217 – 40

20
892 – 70

21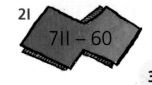
711 – 60

Subtracting multiples of 10

Write the number of minutes left for each film.

1. $116 - 30 = 86$ minutes

1 116 minutes
watched 30 minutes

2 121 minutes
watched 40 minutes

3 119 minutes
watched 50 minutes

4 127 minutes
watched 1 hour

5 142 minutes
watched $1\frac{1}{2}$ hours

6 123 minutes
watched 70 minutes

7 122 minutes
watched 30 minutes

8 132 minutes
watched 50 minutes

9 118 minutes
watched 1 hour

Take each orange number from each green number.

$243 - 60 = 183$

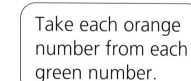

243

70

80

418

60

332

34

Copy and complete.

	–	2 4 1	3 2 1
3 0 2	1 1	2 9 1	

–	241	321	106	445	211
30					
60					
80					
20					

1 Jane has saved **£123**.

She buys a walkman for **£40** and **2** tapes for **£10** each.

How much has she left?

2 Grandad is **107** years old!

He married grandma **70** years ago. How old was he?

They went to America **30** years ago. How old was he then?

Problems

3 Matty has a **500** piece puzzle.

He has put **90** pieces together.

How many are left?

His sister does another **80** pieces.

How much is left to do?

4 **578** people are at the local football match.

At half-time **80** people go home. How many are left?

50 more people leave when it rains. How many are left?

35

Subtracting

155 160 165 170 175 180 185 190 195 200

150
145
140
135
130
125
120
115
110
105
100
95
90
85
80
75
70
65
60
55
50

Copy and complete.

Use the number line.

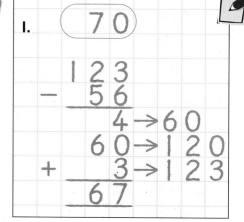

I. 70

```
   1 2 3
 -   5 6
         4 → 6 0
        6 0 → 1 2 0
 +       3 → 1 2 3
        6 7
```

1 123 – 56   **2** 173 – 88

3 142 – 65   **4** 214 – 178   **5** 123 – 76   **6** 122 – 67

7 204 – 166   **8** 214 – 155   **9** 184 – 95   **10** 133 – 74

11 311 – 294   **12** 177 – 67   **13** 405 – 328   **14** 338 – 282

Each film has 38 minutes of adverts and trailers.

Subtract to find how long the actual film is.

?

15

121 minutes

16

126 minutes

17

132 minutes

18

144 minutes

19

137 minutes

20

118 minutes

Subtracting

Write how many boys in each crowd.

1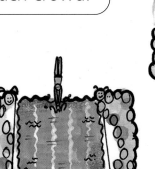
114 children
65 are girls

1. 40

```
    1 1 4
  -   6 5
        5 → 7 0
       3 0 → 1 0 0
  +    1 4 → 1 1 4
       4 9
```

2
186 children
71 are girls

3
223 children
126 are girls

4
119 children
47 are girls

5
253 children
198 are girls

6
207 children
114 are girls

7
245 children
133 are girls

8
118 children
53 are girls

9
302 children
213 are girls

Copy and complete.

10   243 – 167

11   314 – 268   **12**   417 – 347   **13**   624 – 586

14   709 – 644   **15**   313 – 277   **16**   424 – 386

17   503 – 479   **18**   257 – 134   **19**   303 – 223

Two families meet at the beach.

Write how much further one family has driven.

157 miles
343 miles

```
I.    3 4 3      ( 2 0 0 )
    - 1 5 7
           3 → 1 6 0
          40 → 2 0 0
    + 1 4 3 → 3 4 3
      1 8 6 miles
```

2

241 miles
173 miles

3

411 miles
274 miles

4

236 miles
91 miles

5

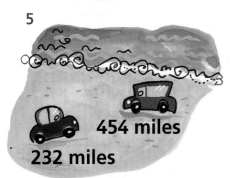

454 miles
232 miles

6

318 miles
107 miles

7

413 miles
102 miles

❷ How far did each pair of families drive in total?

Explore

Use the cards shown.

Make two 3-digit numbers.

Find the difference.

Repeat, making different numbers.

What is the largest and smallest difference you can find?

What is the nearest difference to 400 you can find?

Subtracting

Copy and complete.

1.
```
   H  T  U
   3  4  6
-  1  2  9
_____
```

1. 220
```
   H  T  U
   3³ 4̶ ¹6
-  1  2  9
_____
   2  1  7
```

2.
```
   H  T  U
   5  3  7
-  1  6  2
_____
```

3.
```
   H  T  U
   3  4  1
-  2  2  5
_____
```

4.
```
   H  T  U
   4  6  3
-  2  4  5
_____
```

5.
```
   H  T  U
   4  7  1
-  3  2  2
_____
```

6.
```
   H  T  U
   5  6  4
-  1  2  7
_____
```

7.
```
   H  T  U
   5  6  2
-  2  2  6
_____
```

8.
```
   H  T  U
   6  7  2
-  3  4  8
_____
```

9.
```
   H  T  U
   3  7  2
-  1  4  8
_____
```

10.
```
   H  T  U
   2  7  3
-  1  2  9
_____
```

11.
```
   H  T  U
   6  1  4
-  3  7  2
_____
```

12.
```
   H  T  U
   7  2  7
-  3  6  6
_____
```

13.
```
   H  T  U
   9  1  2
-  4  3  1
_____
```

14.
```
   H  T  U
   5  0  4
-  2  7  1
_____
```

15.
```
   H  T  U
   4  5  6
-  2  7  1
_____
```

16.
```
   H  T  U
   3  3  2
-  1  7  0
_____
```

17.
```
   H  T  U
   4  0  6
-  2  8  2
_____
```

Subtract each blue number from each orange number.

814

459

943

367

188

721

Subtracting

Write how many red fish in each shoal.

1

336 fish
183 blue fish

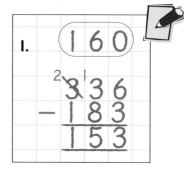
1.
$$\begin{array}{r} \boxed{1\ 6\ 0} \\ \overset{2}{3}\overset{1}{3}6 \\ -\ 1\ 8\ 3 \\ \hline 1\ 5\ 3 \end{array}$$

2

528 fish
262 yellow fish

3

328 fish
191 grey fish

4
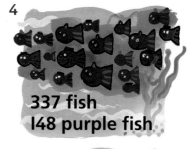
337 fish
148 purple fish

5
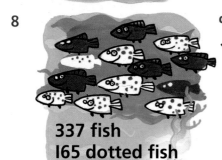
347 fish
158 pink fish

6

364 fish
192 blue fish

7
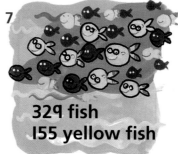
329 fish
155 yellow fish

8

337 fish
165 dotted fish

9

403 fish
181 striped fish

10
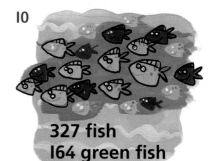
327 fish
164 green fish

Write the difference between the number of each type of fish in each shoal.

1a
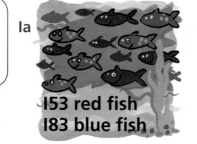
153 red fish
183 blue fish

1a.
$$\begin{array}{r} H\ T\ U \\ 1\ 8\ 3 \\ -\ 1\ 5\ 3 \\ \hline 3\ 0 \end{array}$$

Subtracting

> Write the new weights.

1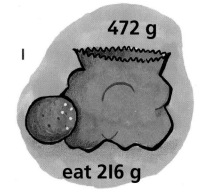

472 g

eat 216 g

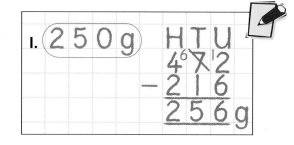

1. 250 g

```
    H T U
    4⁶7¹2
  -  2 1 6
     2 5 6 g
```

2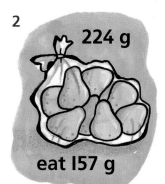

224 g

eat 157 g

3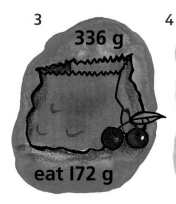

336 g

eat 172 g

4

417 g

eat 208 g

5

293 g

eat 144 g

6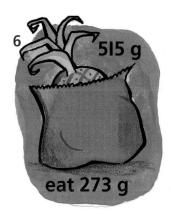

515 g

eat 273 g

7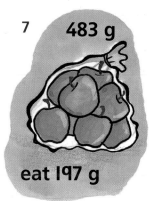

483 g

eat 197 g

8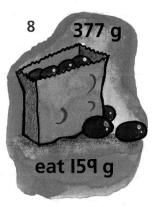

377 g

eat 159 g

9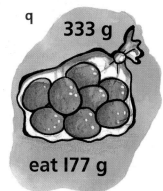

333 g

eat 177 g

Problems

10 There are **237** children in the school.

128 are girls.

How many boys are there?

11 The school has **176** days holiday each year.

There are **365** days in a year.

How many days do the children go to school?

Odd and even

Copy and write 'odd' or 'even' beside each number.

1  472

1. 4 7 2 even

2 555

3  641

4  229

5  318

6  744

7  908

8  163

9  227

10  842

11  669

12  343

13  516

14  732

Write the next 2 even numbers.

15  78

15. 7 8, 8 0, 8 2

16  116

17  310

18  968

19  196

20  438

21  514

22  666

23  798

24  444

25  396

26  108

27  998

ℯ Write the previous 2 even numbers in each chain.

Odd and even

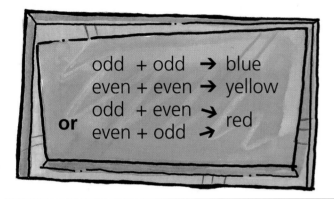

Copy and complete this addition table.

Colour the answers as follows:

odd + odd	→	blue
even + even	→	yellow
odd + even	→	red
or even + odd	→	

+	1	2	3	4	5	6
1			4			
2						
3		5				
4				8		
5	6					
6			9			

What do you notice?

Write odd or even.

1 7 + 9

1. 7 + 9, even

2 5 + 6

3 23 + 37

4 42 + 54

5 16 + 12

6 54 + 17

7 513 + 123

8 138 + 223

9 565 + 363

Explore

Copy the grid. Write touching pairs with an even total.

How many can you find?

Find touching pairs with an odd total.

3	8	1
2	7	5
4	9	6

4 + 2 = 6
7 + 1 = 8

Odd and even

Copy and complete this subtraction table.

Colour the answers as follows:

	odd – odd	→	blue
	even – even	→	yellow
or	odd – even	→	red
	even – odd	→	

What do you notice?

−	7	8	9	10	11	12
1	6					
2					9	
3						
4			5			
5						
6				4		

Calculate each child's winnings.

Subtract one number from the other on each ticket.

Even answers win £1·00.   Odd answers win 50p.

1. Bob
$$15 - 9 = 6$$
$$24 - 12 = 12$$
$$8 - 7 = 1$$
$$£1 + £1 + 50p = £2·50$$

1 Bob   15 9   8 7   24 12

2 Sanjit   13 7   12 8   18 9

3 Jenna   9 3   11 6   21 14

4 Tim   11 2   24 6   17 9

5 Jo   18 12   22 18   16 9

Negative numbers

Write the temperature shown.

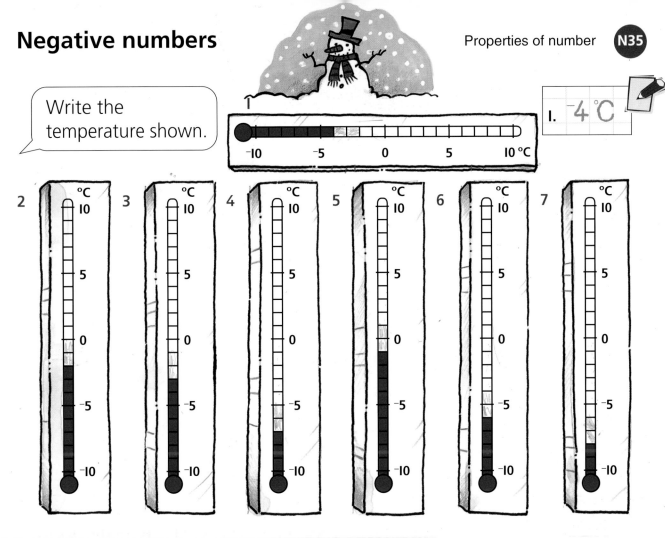

1. ⁻4°C

8. ⁻6°C

The temperature goes up 2°C. Write the new temperature.

The temperature drops 9°C one night.

Write the new temperature in each place.

Negative numbers

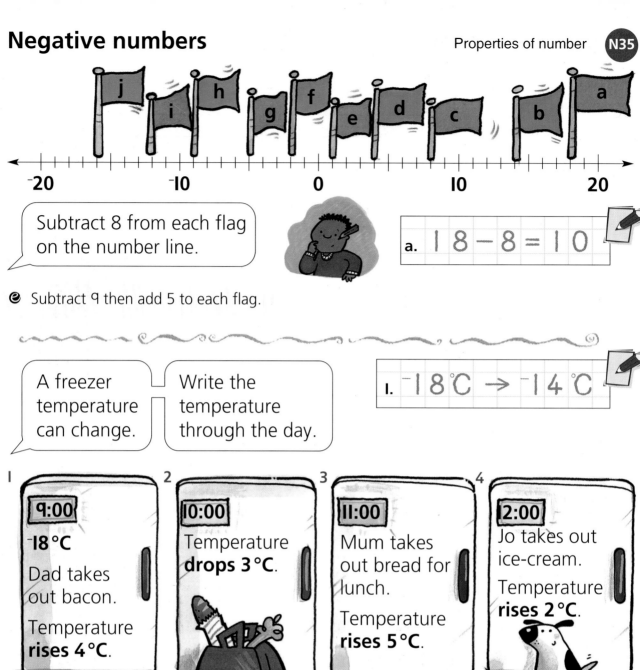

Subtract 8 from each flag on the number line.

a. $18 - 8 = 10$

☉ Subtract 9 then add 5 to each flag.

A freezer temperature can change.

Write the temperature through the day.

I. $^-18\,°C \rightarrow {}^-14\,°C$

1 9:00
$^-18\,°C$

Dad takes out bacon.

Temperature **rises 4 °C**.

2 10:00
Temperature **drops 3 °C**.

3 11:00
Mum takes out bread for lunch.

Temperature **rises 5 °C**.

4 2:00
Jo takes out ice-cream.

Temperature **rises 2 °C**.

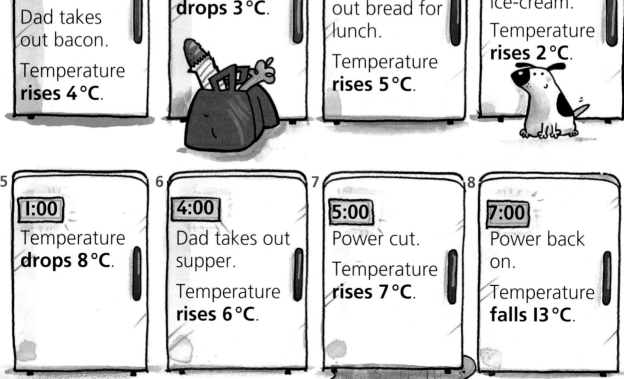

5 1:00
Temperature **drops 8 °C**.

6 4:00
Dad takes out supper.

Temperature **rises 6 °C**.

7 5:00
Power cut.
Temperature **rises 7 °C**.

8 7:00
Power back on.

Temperature **falls 13 °C**.

Negative numbers

Write how much each child still owes.

1 Sam

has 15p
owes 20p

1. $15 - 20 = -5$
Sam still owes 5 p.

2 Lily

has 12p
owes 15p

3 Chuy

has 10p
owes 20p

4 Bill

has 8p
owes 13p

5 Simone

has 11p
owes 17p

6 Jon

has 12p
owes 21p

7 Hatti

has 23p
owes 27p

8 Samira

has 45p
owes 51p

9 Dan

has 14p
owes 32p

10 Amrita

has 7p
owes 12p

11 Jack

has 9p
owes 20p

12 Mel

has 22p
owes 33p

13 Vikram

has 14p
owes 32p

Explore

Use a red dice for ⊕ numbers.

Use a blue dice for ⊖ numbers.

How many different pairs of dice numbers can you make with a score of ⁻1?

$4 + -5 = -1$

Doubling

Write the weight for the pair of shoes.

I

360 g

I. double 3 6 0

600 + 120 = 720 g

2

240 g

3

310 g

4

170 g

5

380 g

6

460 g

7

190 g

Write the total number of steps up and down.

8

240 steps up

8. double 2 4 0

400 + 80 = 480

q

330 steps up

10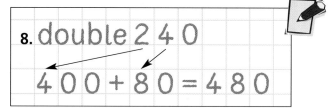

260 steps up

11

470 steps up

12

180 steps up

13

250 steps up

14

390 steps up

Halving

The distance shows there and back.

Write how far away the object is.

1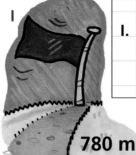
780 m

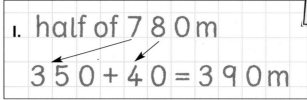
I. half of 780m
350 + 40 = 390m

2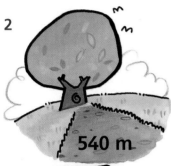
540 m

3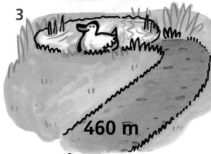
460 m

4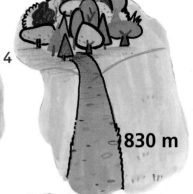
830 m

5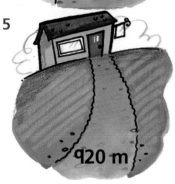
920 m

6
340 m

7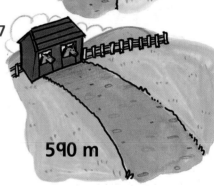
590 m

Flight tickets are half-price.

Write the new cost.

8
Florida
£580

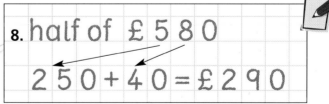
8. half of £580
250 + 40 = £290

9
Bali
£760

10
California
£440

11
Gran Canaria
£320

12
Singapore
£650

13
Sydney
£940

14
Greece
£380

Doubling and halving

Giant Soup

Ingredients

3400 potatoes
4600 carrots
1800 onions
2700 tomatoes
2100 celery sticks
440   pints of stock

Serves 1000 people

Write the ingredients for:

1 2000 people

2 500 people   3 250 people

Copy and complete each table.

in	out
2300	4600

double

in	out
2300	
4500	
1700	
480	
3700	
290	
3100	

halve

in	out
6800	
780	
4900	
2700	
8600	
930	
5800	

Multiplying

The people are sitting in rows.

Write how many people in total.

1

4 rows of 22

```
I.    80
      22
   ×   4
   ─────
       8    4 × 2
   + 80     4 × 20
   ─────
      88
```

2

3 rows of 12

3

2 rows of 32

4

3 rows of 15

5

5 rows of 14

6

2 rows of 35

7

4 rows of 38

8

2 rows of 56

9

3 rows of 29

10

7 rows of 45

Copy and complete.

```
11   27        12   15
   ×  5           ×  4
```

```
13   21     14   32     15   51     16   28
   ×  5        ×  5        ×  4        ×  5
```

```
II.   150
       27
    ×   5
    ─────
       35    5 × 7
   + 100     5 × 20
   ──────
     135
```

```
17   43     18   37     19   35     20   62
   ×  6        ×  4        ×  7        ×  5
```

Multiplying

 banana 14p

 pineapple 42p

 mango 31p

 orange 26p

 apple 18p

Write the total cost.

1 **5 mangoes**

2 **4 oranges**

3 **5 apples**

```
1.  (150p)
      3 1
    ×   5
    ─────
        5    5 × 1
  + 1 5 0    5 × 30
  ─────────
    1 5 5 p = £ 1·5 5
```

4 **6 pineapples**

5 **7 oranges**

6 **8 mangoes**

7 **7 bananas**

 13p each

 21p each

 32p each

 28p each

 43p each

Write the total cost.

8 **6 glue sticks**

```
8.  (180p)
      3 2
    ×   6
    ─────
      1 2    6 × 2
  + 1 8 0    6 × 30
  ─────────
    1 9 2 p = £ 1·9 2
```

9 **5 crayons**

10 **4 rulers**

11 **6 pencils**

12 **8 crayons**

13 **7 glue sticks**

14 **4 pens**

Multiplying

Write the perimeter of each pool.

All pool shapes are regular.

1

← 23 m →

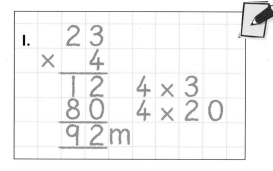

```
      2 3
  ×     4
      1 2    4 × 3
      8 0    4 × 20
      9 2 m
```

2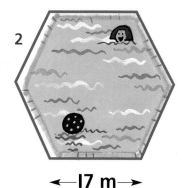

← 17 m →

3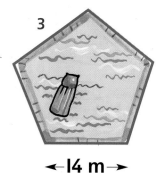

← 14 m →

4

← 22 m →

5

13 m

6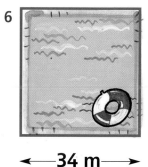

← 34 m →

7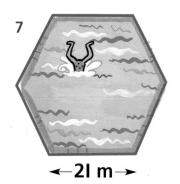

← 21 m →

8

← 49 m →

🄴 Draw some pools of your own and write the perimeters.

Explore

Use the cards shown.

Arrange any 3 to make a multiplication.

What are the largest and smallest possible products (answers)?

How many different products (answers) can you find?

Divide each amount between 10 children.

Write how much is left over.

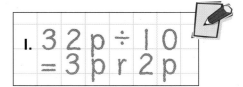

I. $32p \div 10$
$= 3p \ r \ 2p$

1

32p

2

44p

3
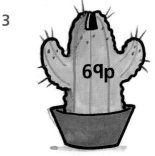
69p

4

71p

5

83p

6

104p

7

67p

8

70p

9

58p

e   Choose 5 more amounts and divide them by 10.

Copy and complete.

Use tables lists.

10. $46 \div 5 = 9 \ r \ 1$

10   $46 \div 5 =$

11   $13 \div 3 =$

12   $11 \div 2 =$

13   $37 \div 5 =$

14   $21 \div 2 =$

15   $16 \div 5 =$

16   $23 \div 3 =$

17   $28 \div 5 =$

18   $25 \div 2 =$

Dividing

I. $22 \div 5 = 4 \text{ r } 2$
r = 2 bones

Divide the bones between 5 dogs. | Write how many are left over.

1
22 bones

2
43 bones

3
31 bones

4
29 bones

5
17 bones

6
58 bones

7
42 bones

8
64 bones

9
75 bones

Copy and complete. | Use tables lists. | 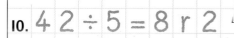 10. $42 \div 5 = 8 \text{ r } 2$

10    $42 \div 5 =$

11    $20 \div 6 =$

12    $38 \div 9 =$

13    $33 \div 8 =$

14    $28 \div 3 =$

15    $49 \div 6 =$

16    $15 \div 4 =$

17    $43 \div 8 =$

18    $66 \div 9 =$

Dividing

1 Each tube holds **5** tennis balls.

There are **42** balls.

How many tubes are needed?

Problems

2 Tickets to the fun park cost **£5**.

How many tickets can Mum buy with **£47**?

3 At the party there are **6** cakes on each plate.

There are **7** plates and **3** cakes left over.

How many cakes?

4 There are **47** players in the football club.

They are put into teams of **7**.

How many players are not in a team?

Divide these 28 balls between:

5 3 girls   6 2 boys

5. $28 \div 3 = 9 \text{ r } 1$

7 8 dogs   8 9 cats   9 5 dads   10 6 mums   11 7 footballers

Explore

4 divides into 20 exactly.

Which other numbers divide into 20 exactly?

$20 \div 4 = 5$

Find numbers that divide exactly into:

12   30   24

Dividing

Some children are going on a train journey.

Write how many groups go on each journey.

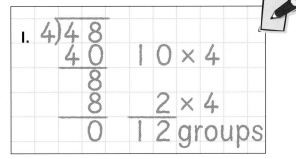

```
1.  4)4 8
       4 0     1 0 × 4
         8
         8     2 × 4
         0     1 2 groups
```

1

48 children sitting in 4s

2

24 children sitting in 2s

3
36 children sitting in 2s

4
39 children sitting in 3s

5
64 children sitting in 4s

6
69 children sitting in 3s

7
85 children sitting in 5s

8
57 children sitting in 3s

9
76 children sitting in 4s

Copy and complete.

10 2)32

11 3)69

```
10.  2)3 2
        2 0     1 0 × 2
          1 2
          1 2     6 × 2
           0     1 6
```

12 5)85

13 4)68

14 2)48

15 6)78

16 6)96

17 7)91

18 5)65

19 3)96

20 7)98

21 4)76

Dividing

The batteries fit different torches.

Write how many torches will work with each set.

$$
\begin{array}{r}
1. \quad 4)\overline{5\,2} \\
\underline{4\,0} \quad 10 \times 4 \\
1\,2 \\
\underline{1\,2} \quad 3 \times 4 \\
0 \quad \overline{13}
\end{array}
$$

1
52 batteries
4 in a torch

2
63 batteries
3 in a torch
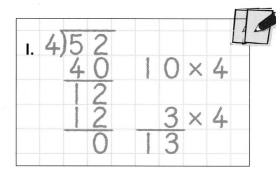

3
78 batteries
6 in a torch

4
84 batteries
4 in a torch
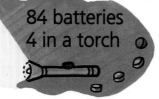

5
72 batteries
3 in a torch

6
66 batteries
3 in a torch

7
84 batteries
4 in a torch

8
84 batteries
6 in a torch
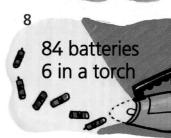

9
93 batteries
3 in a torch

10
64 batteries
2 in a torch

11
72 batteries
3 in a torch

Copy and complete.

12 $2)\overline{88}$

$$
\begin{array}{r}
12. \quad 2)\overline{8\,8} \\
\underline{8\,0} \quad 40 \times 2 \\
8 \\
\underline{8} \quad 4 \times 2 \\
0 \quad \overline{44}
\end{array}
$$

13 $3)\overline{48}$

14 $4)\overline{72}$

15 $5)\overline{75}$

16 $2)\overline{74}$

17 $3)\overline{87}$

18 $4)\overline{64}$

19 $3)\overline{75}$

20 $2)\overline{92}$

21 $3)\overline{81}$

22 $3)\overline{93}$

Dividing

1 Jake has **84** cards.

They are sold in packs of **4**.

How many packs can be made?

2 **3** brothers have **£96**.

They share it equally.

How much do they have each?

Problems

3 Tom spent **65p** on crayons.

They are **5p** each.

How many did he buy?

4 Gemma has **96 cm** of ribbon.

She cuts it into **6** equal pieces.

How long is each piece?

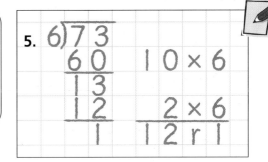

The fruit bars are packed in boxes.

Write how many boxes for each set.

Write how many bars are left over.

5. $6 \overline{)73}$
      60   10×6
      13
      12   2×6
       1      $12 \, r \, 1$

5 73 bars
6 in a box

6 66 bars
4 in a box

7 81 bars
7 in a box

8 47 bars
3 in a box

9 58 bars
4 in a box

 Explore

Which number between 50 and 100, leaves a remainder of 1 when divided by 2, 3, 4, 5 and 6?

Write the fraction coloured green.

I

I. $\dfrac{3}{10}$

2

3

4

5

6

7

8

q

10

Ia. $\dfrac{3}{10} = 0.3$

Write each fraction as a decimal.

Write the position of each worm.

a 0·4 m

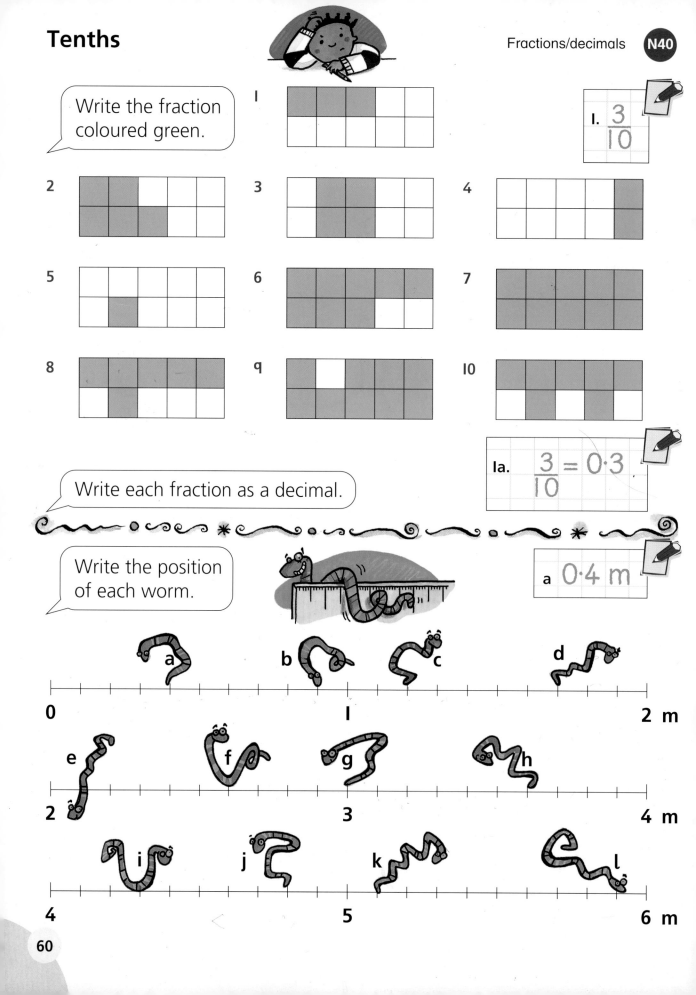

Tenths

Write the letter that matches each number.

1. **4·6**

1. **h** _____

a b c d e

3 4 5 6

f g h i

2. **4·4**   3. **3·3**   4. **6·0**   5. **3·5**

6. **5·4**   7. **3·8**   8. **4·9**   9. **3·9**

Write each weight.

10.

2   3
kg

10. **2·4 kg**

11.
3   4
kg

12.
2   3
kg

13.
1   2
kg

14.
3   4
kg

15.
4   5
kg

16.
0   1
kg

61

Write the weights in order from smallest to largest.

I·I kg
I·3 kg

4·2 kg

I·I kg

4·0 kg

2·6 kg

I·7 kg

3·9 kg

I·3 kg

5·3 kg

3·6 kg

4·7 kg

2·9 kg

5·I kg

Explore

Use the number cards shown.

Use 2 cards to make different decimal numbers.

How many can you make?

Write them in order from smallest to largest.

5   3   2

5·3
5·2

Hundredths

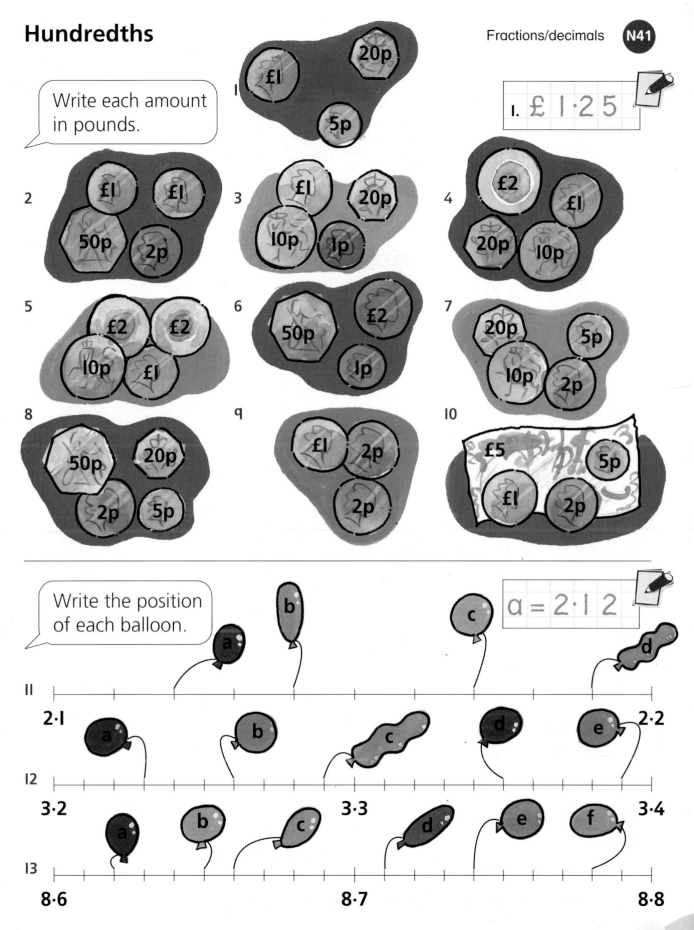

Write each amount in pounds.

1. £1·25

1. £1 20p 5p

2. £1 £1 50p 2p

3. £1 20p 10p 1p

4. £2 £1 20p 10p

5. £2 £2 10p £1

6. 50p £2 1p

7. 20p 5p 10p 2p

8. 50p 20p 2p 5p

9. £1 2p 2p

10. £5 5p £1 2p

Write the position of each balloon.

a = 2·12

11.
a b c d

12.
2·1 a b c d e 2·2

13.
3·2 a b c d e f 3·4
3·3

8·6   8·7   8·8

63

Write each length in metres.

I 2 m 25 cm

I. 2·25 m

2 I m 32 cm

3 I m 20 cm

4 I30 cm

5 $\frac{1}{2}$ m

6 45 cm

7 256 cm

8 3 m 60 cm

q 4 $\frac{1}{2}$ m

I0 I $\frac{1}{4}$ m

Write the letter to match each number.

II. k

II 4·25

a b c d e f

4·0   4·1   4·2   4·3

g h i j k

I2 4·I9   **I3** 4·I3   **I4** 4·27   **I5** 4·09   **I6** 4·02

I7 4·I5   **I8** 4·04   **I9** 4·I8   **20** 4·07   **2I** 4·22

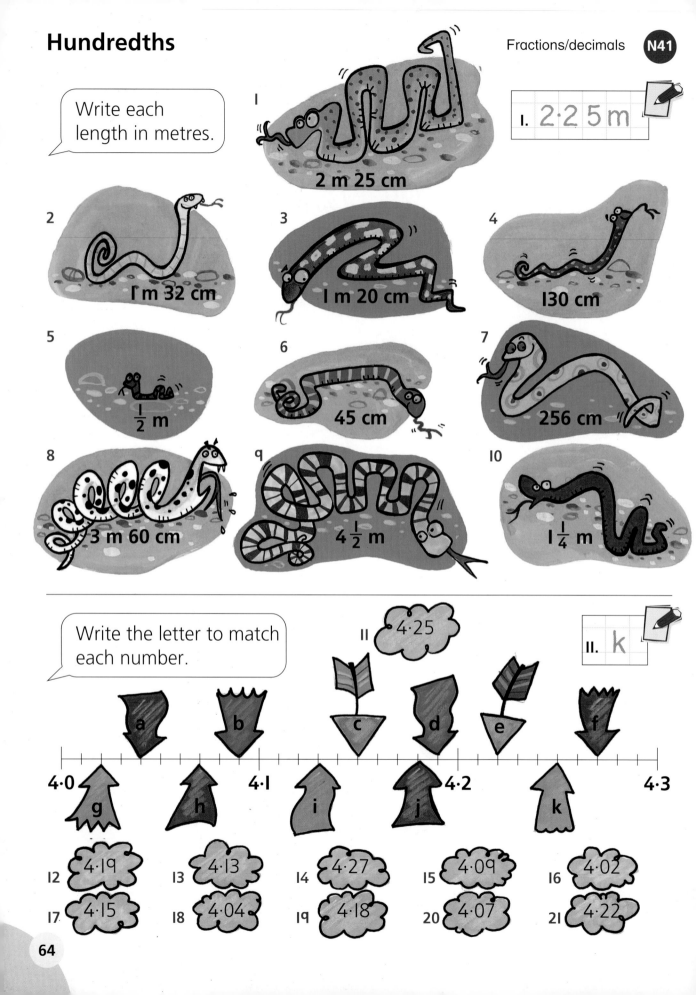

Each price goes up by 1p. | Write the new price.

I. £3·16

1. £3·17

2  £5·14

3  £1·17

4  £3·39

5  £4·99

6  £3·04

7  £6·99

8  £7·80

9  £1·90

10  £7·00

11  £8·02

12 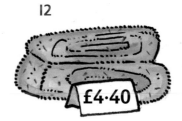 £4·40

13  £1·82

Each price goes down by 1p. | Write the new price.

14. £8·80

14  £8·81

15  £7·02

16  £4·98

17  £5·10

18  £9·80

19  £3·00

20  £3·90

21  £4·49

Subtracting

Take away the amount shown.

take away 257

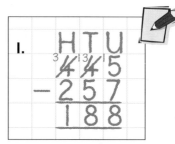

I.
```
      H  T  U
      3 ¹³ ¹
      4  4  5
   -  2  5  7
   ────────────
      1  8  8
```

2
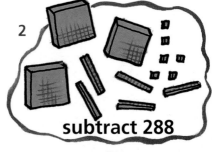

subtract 288

3

minus 159

4

258 less

5

take away 289

6

97 less

7
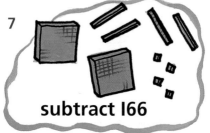

subtract 166

8

minus 157

9
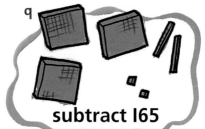

subtract 165

10
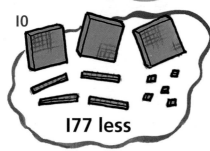

177 less

Copy and complete.

II.
```
   H  T  U
   5  6  4
-  2  8  7
```

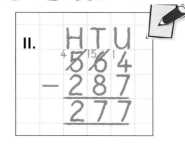

II.
```
      H  T  U
      4 ¹⁵ ¹
      5  6  4
   -  2  8  7
   ────────────
      2  7  7
```

12
```
   H  T  U
   4  7  3
-  2  9  6
```

13
```
   H  T  U
   8  8  5
-  2  9  7
```

14
```
   H  T  U
   6  6  4
-  4  8  8
```

15
```
   H  T  U
   8  3  7
-  4  7  8
```

66

Subtracting

The race is 911 km long.

Write how far each car still has to go.

```
      H T U
    8
    9̶ 1 1
  - 2 8 1
    6 3 0  km
```
1.

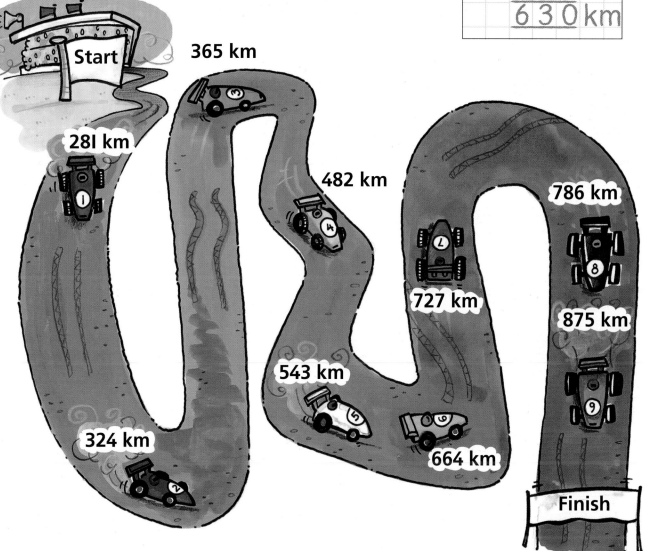

Start

365 km

281 km

482 km

786 km

727 km

875 km

543 km

324 km

664 km

Finish

Take each green number away from each orange number.

716

345

```
      H T U
    6 1
    7̶ 1̶ 6
  - 3 4 5
    3 7 1
```

924

488

698

833

Subtracting

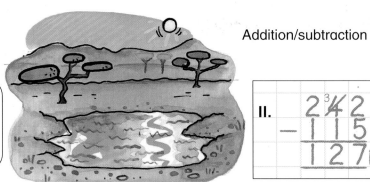

Write how far each animal has to go to reach the water hole.

II.
$$\begin{array}{r} 2\,{}^{3}\!\!\!\!4\,2 \\ -\ 1\ 1\ 5 \\ \hline 1\ 2\ 7\,m \end{array}$$

I
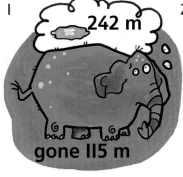
242 m
gone 115 m

2

621 m
gone 136 m

3
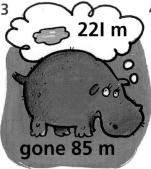
221 m
gone 85 m

4
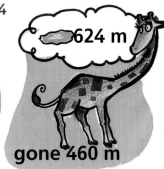
624 m
gone 460 m

5

213 m
gone 124 m

6

321 m
gone 236 m

7

263 m
gone 172 m

8

305 m
gone 218 m

9
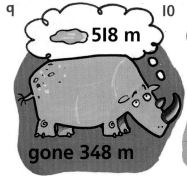
518 m
gone 348 m

10

646 m
gone 527 m

11

685 m
gone 658 m

12
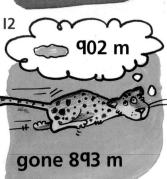
902 m
gone 893 m

 **Explore**

Write 2 numbers.

BUT … the difference between them must be:

- a 3-digit number
- a number with consecutive digits, e.g. 123, 456, …

Write several pairs.

$$\begin{array}{r} 5\ {}^{6}\!\!\!7\ {}^{1}\!2 \\ -\ 4\ 4\ 9 \\ \hline 1\ 2\ 3 \end{array}$$

68

Adding and subtracting

Write the total cost for each pair of CDs.

1  £4·87 £5·68

```
     £ 5 . 6 8
1. + £ 4 . 8 7
   £ 1 0 . 5 5
        1 1
```

2  £13·58 £7·77

3  £15·49 £12·75

4  £9·99 £11·11

5  £4·75 £3·86

6  £10·49 £12·87

7  £9·87 £13·56

8  £9·19 £7·77

9  £11·29 £14·98

10  £8·76 £12·41

Write the difference between each pair of numbers.

11  £2·22 £4·11

```
     £ 4 . 1 1
II. - £ 2 . 2 2
    £ 1 . 8 9
```

12  £3·50 £1·75

13 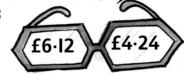 £6·12 £4·24

14  £4·20 £1·80

15  £3·17 £1·77

16  £2·80 £1·90

Subtracting

Write how much more the larger plant costs.

1.

$$\begin{array}{r} £2\overset{2}{3}\cdot\overset{1}{2}9 \\ -£1\cdot79 \\ \hline £1\cdot50 \end{array}$$

1 £3·29   £1·79

2 £5·59   £3·89

3 £6·38   £2·98

4 £4·37   £1·67

5 £10·16   £2·96

6 £5·29   £2·79

7 £1·46   £8·16

8 £7·57   £3·87

9 £2·76   £4·26

10 £3·98   £6·28

Write the pairs of numbers with a difference of £1·99.

?

£4·68   £3·73   £9·98   £5·55   £6·67   £3·36   £7·54   £5·35   £1·74   £7·99

Subtracting

Write how much each child must save.

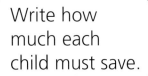

1.

$$\begin{array}{r} £19.99 \\ - £8.78 \\ \hline £11.21 \end{array}$$

2 £10·19

3 £11·12

4 £5·50

5 £13·75

6 £13·64

7 £11·79

8 £15·75

Special offer

Best game ever

£19.99

GALAXY WARS

Explore

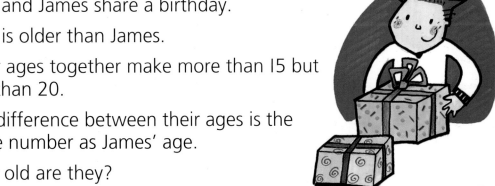

Jane and James share a birthday.

Jane is older than James.

Their ages together make more than 15 but less than 20.

The difference between their ages is the same number as James' age.

How old are they?

Mixed problems

1  Simon has run **346 m**.

He runs another **168 m**.

 How much further to reach his **1 km** target?

2 Megan had **4** puppies.

These are the puppies' weights when born.

346 g 425 g
475 g 582 g

Find the total weight.

They **double** in weight after 2 weeks.

What is the total weight now?

3a Jinda scores **468**.

Mark scores **512**.

How much more has Mark scored?

b Jinda scores **275** more.

Mark scores **196** more.

Who is the winner and by how much?

c Jinda crashes. She loses **500** points.

Mark blew up his castle. He lost **400** points.

What is the final score for each of them?

4

SCARY MOVIE £14·49
THE WESTERN £12·99
SHARK ATTACK £11·69
ACTION £10·89
SPOOKY
Monkey Business £13·79
£9·69

a Which **3** videos can Ben buy with **£38·50** and leave the least change?

b If Ben had **£45**, could he buy **4** videos?